Mud Song

WINNER OF THE 2017 T. S. ELIOT PRIZE

The T. S. Eliot Prize for Poetry is an annual award sponsored by Truman State University Press for the best unpublished book-length collection of poetry in English, in honor of native Missourian T. S. Eliot's considerable intellectual and artistic legacy.

Judge for 2017: Kevin Prufer

Mud Song

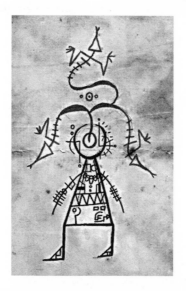

Terry Ann Thaxton

New Odyssey
Truman State University Press
Kirksville, Missouri

Cover art: *The Fishers*, original artwork by Adam Thaxton.
Cover design: Lisa Ahrens

Section pages: Original artwork by Adam Thaxton.

Library of Congress Cataloging-in-Publication Data

Names: Thaxton, Terry Ann, author.
Title: Mud song / by Terry Ann Thaxton.
Description: Kirksville, Missouri : Truman State University Press, 2017. |
  Series: New Odyssey series | Includes bibliographical references and index.
Identifiers: LCCN 2017019424 (print) | LCCN 2017019647 (ebook) | ISBN
  9781612482170 | ISBN 9781612482163 (pbk. : alk. paper)
Classification: LCC PS3620.H38 (ebook) | LCC PS3620.H38 A6 2017 (print) |
  DDC 811/.6—dc23
LC record available at https://lccn.loc.gov/2017019424

For my son, Adam,
sixth-generation Floridian

"The general wildness, the eternal labyrinths of waters and marshes, interlocked and apparently never ending; the whole surrounded by interminable swamps. . . . Here I am then in the Floridas, thought I."

—John James Audubon (letter to the editor of *Monthly American Journal of Geology and Natural Science*, 1831)

Contents

Part Three

Part Four

Part Five

Postlude

Acknowledgements | *79*

Prelude

History of America

On the boat the men drank whatever the women poured
while the women buoyed up the heads of sick children,
and then they were peeling corn, and potatoes rose from
the earth. I never paid attention in school. Didn't understand

the purpose of history. Or science. Women sharpened knives
not knowing they could be used against them. There was a table
and probably not a turkey—which is something I learned
only recently. And then some men fought with swords.

It all started at a rock. Then some guy with white hair wrote out
his hope for his neighbors, absent of a queen hovering over
his bookshelf. There might have been women, too, who wanted
to wear their dresses as short as I did when I was a young girl.

But it wasn't until the 1800s when I started paying attention,
and only because of a small cabin in the woods built
by a man who wanted nothing to do with this country. There
were women who hid words in their panties drawer, words

not discovered until they were dead, like witches flying above a man
ashamed of his own past. After the rock, our ancestors dispersed
into the wild west where whores sprouted from behind rocks and men
of course had to pay to see breasts, and so guns were created to save

our freedom. My sixth-grade teacher taped the evolution poster
to our classroom door—but only because, she said, the county
forced her to. Otherwise, I would never have seen the parade of apes,
the men, following each other into history.

Part One

Alligators

:1997:

Mating season is April. I come home
one afternoon, and a neighbor stops me
before I pull into my driveway. *There's one
in your front flower bed*, he says.
It's a twelve-footer,
lounging between the bottlebrush tree and
azaleas. The trapper nooses it, and it twists
on the ground like a blender.
When it tires, the trapper covers its eyes with
duct tape, then tapes its legs to its body.
Four men load it into the truck.
They promise to take it to a bigger lake.

:1974:

We were fifteen. Jill was tired
of Florida heat, and dove off the dock into the dark
lake at the state park five miles from my house.

:1995:

We sit down at the edge of a quarry in the Everglades,
pull out our sandwiches, our apples, our water bottles.
On the opposite bank one drags itself
into the water and heads toward us.

:2007:

A different house, and one moseys
from the small pond out back
through my side yard
and my husband goes out to stop it
from heading across the street
where two young children
are splashing with their grandmother

in her pool. I run over to warn them.
Do you want to go see it? she asks the kids.
As if this might be entertainment.

:1976:

Dad swings the sickle to rid one end
of our pond of weeds.
We know that end holds their babies.
She leaps from the water
toward my brother. I watch from the riding mower
as the mother alligator chases him. Dad yells,
jumps toward it with his sickle.
Mother comes out with a shotgun, shoots it
between the eyes.

:: ::

In dreams I'm stepping through the shallow end of a pond
or swimming in a big lake and only when
I'm surrounded do I realize how many there are below and beside me.

Afternoon Forecast

This summer it has rained every afternoon, right on schedule,
just as it did when you and I drove into strange driveways

to pick up clothes for Cubans who had drifted to Florida on rafts,
looking for a new life. Mother, in the years since your death,

I've wanted to write to you in your palace of dirt,
and tell you the story of my life, and now, I finally can:

I've moved the gardenia bush to the other side of the yard
for sunlight. In its place, beneath the shade of an overbearing

camphor tree, I buried the roots of a canna lily, and just outside
my window I can watch its petals fall onto the wet earth.

From that window, the dog from next door watches me, and,
like me when I tried to talk to you, she whines and sighs,

knowing that I will never understand what she really wants. Perhaps
it is so: when you were alive, you dusted the air between us

with your secrets, and now we are barely part of the same earth.
Why is it, Mother, that even though I have planted everything

I had ever hoped to plant, the gardenia will not put forth white flowers?
Sometimes it is too much for one woman, and then I remember

that you never found the sky empty of rain clouds either.
I am doing good deeds, as you taught me, even though, unlike you,

I know it will not get me any closer to your god or keep me out
of hell. I can still imagine the people of the second exodus that you rescued,

the clothes you gathered for them: house after house, the rain beating
on windowed lives, you stood at the doorbell while my eyes

peeked through the Florida afternoon storm. I can see you,
oh Mary, oh Rescuer of Barren Lives, swimming back, climbing on board,

with me in the learner's seat, ferrying the dejected clothes to churches
for distribution. Nothing has changed, Mary: people are still hoping

they can live inside someone else's clothes, like me, like the dead leaf
outside my window, holding on to the thread of an abandoned spider's web.

The Dog in the Garage

The trees have been hungry in my dreams,
then last night my dog walked through thick mud,

could barely get her paws out, and yesterday when I locked
her in the garage, I did not notice her voice crumbling,

could not hear her paws scratching at the door,
and then I could not explain to her it was a lapse of mind.

I once found sand dollars on the beach, but I did not dance
with the music which I have always called for more sky.

My couch rests along the wall below the bird feeder
hanging outside, the pine cones and feathers

line the windowsill. The crab shell reminds me
of walking through gray mud, and distances.

Florida Survival Guide

Here, even the squirrels know how to peel
an orange. They live, sometimes,
without tails or without feet, pulled off by hawks.

For several years we lived with drought
and the county law of not watering the lawn
except on Thursdays and Sundays.

Now the pond is filled again—water from
three hurricanes in one season, and my yard
is spattered with those gray tails flitting along

aluminum poles that hold the bird feeders
above the wicked middle fingers
of saw palmettos. During the second

hurricane, we hunkered down
in our hallways with candles, flashlights,
and battery-powered radios, waiting to hear

where the eye of the storm would pass,
and I thought about a trail where I once saw
a sinking Chevy pickup truck.

Here, in Florida, you do not need a watch.
Here you begin to understand why the elderly
spend years in the swamp, waiting to wear

the grave's black hair. The night of the first hurricane,
I knew not to be fooled into false security
during the lull of the storm. Days earlier,

we'd bought jugs of water, filled our bathtubs,
emptied food from our refrigerators, and some
of us placed orders across county lines for generators.

The evening before, we moved our cars,
wisely waited in long lines to fill gas tanks.
At home, we gathered candles, brought in

lawn furniture, carried potted plants
into the garage. The morning after, I stepped out
the front door and walked over the limbs,

which the day before had hung high above
my flower bed. On the street:
trees and power poles. Neighbors came out

from under fallen trees, clinging to their own bodies
as if a ghost, without warning, would pull them up
from our muddied street like feathers,

as if their houses could no longer protect them
from this world. We stood in the street, the neighbors
and I, shaking our heads, saying nothing.

Dead Owl

No one understands the sinkhole problem.
I gawk. I keep stones in my ears,
though sometimes I breathe pebbles into tree branches.

I do not know if we should leave it here or take it home,
stuff it, and admire it.

Unless you're dying to preach to me
or swing from the top of the tree house,
don't bother coming to rescue me.

I thought all that was left was ash and bone fragments
and a stranger's black pajamas in the ditch.

The sun burns everything, and my right hand
has slapped a boy's cheek. I sit near
the cloud of discontentment.

I just wanted to hear myself ask the question
about the neighborhood of weak houses.

Each day clings to my jeans.
Each day I have to stomp out my boots on the road.

I laugh because I know I'll die someday too.

The sun takes away the shadows of your eyes.
My head is only present because I recognize the highway.

Each day is an unmarked grave filled with muck and insects.
Sometimes I think I've been away my entire life.

Drought

Rain tempts the lonely throat of day, taunting
each crinkling leaf, like a call girl wearing red pumps

and stockings just outside the car window in a dream.
The clothes in the dryer try to swap themselves

for the men of her past. She knows the house is waiting.
She tells herself she will go out tomorrow as the washing machine

asks her again to reverse the clothes, but she throws dirty shirts
into the rinse cycle. Only the pond behind the house is not

serious, and she thinks of marching toward it,
perhaps reaching a gray cloud, pulling the switch.

Outside, moss hangs itself in trees like fresh-dried laundry,
and she recalls the switches her father ordered her to cut

from the paper tree to spank her for being bad, for being
a girl. Her hair curves into the drought:

twenty wandering summers fall from trees, and inside
one of the summers, a door opens; she grabs a man, says, dance

with me. Those switches still hang in the trees,
and she drags her ass back to the dishes.

Bees hum carefully outside her window.
The rain wishes she were not so desperate.

She reminds herself to throw out history
when she takes out the garbage,

but each time, the saw palmettos snicker at her, and she
never notices how many trees have been sacrificed.

Escape

If you find yourself in the swamp, clap your hands
or wave your feather in the dark and turn your face

toward the tiny cup along the rim, and imagine
rain reaching down like a swing that rescues children

on hot afternoons, careful not to stop boasting about your walk
on the trail where you wanted to crack open a window

as if a toad wanted in, as if it was groaning like a stranger
who swaggers into your head and hides in your sweater

or who wants to fill your mouth with lace because there is
no doubt that you can handle the past the same way you

pour soup or the way a rabbit might gaze at the garden and ignore
the cabbage, and if rain injects the day or your desk harbors

secrets that listen only to the fingers dressing themselves
in afterthought, because it's just as easy to juggle the badges

you imagine to be worn by moths, by then you'll want to
persuade the cemetery to go under, to sniff the dead frogs

that fell from yesterday's rains, or to rush past the field and spread
open the flag, being careful not to vanish when they close the gate.

What Remains

—for Russ

I find oranges just beyond
my dining room window,
fallen from the tree, some half-

eaten by squirrels in the shape
of my mother's memory.
Sometimes I pick up the whole ones,

take my arm, as I did when
I was a girl on first base,
wind up and throw the orange

through bushes and shrubs until it
plops into the pond. The sound
reminds me that there is

an ocean somewhere beyond
the pests in my yard. Sometimes,
only part of the skin

remains, the rest gone,
disappeared, like my mother's
voice hanging on the clothesline.

Sometimes I'm sure I'm almost
there, but she made her escape
like an angel or an orchid

on my back porch, having
remained in bloom longer
than anyone in our house expected.

Some people say Florida
looks like a flower. I say, come, trace
my foot—I'll try to show you

how to live after your mother leaves you,
as if we, the living, were something
more solid than antique china

on a shelf in a woman's pantry.
The story is never over.

Road Rage

The county is widening the road
near my house from two to four lanes.
Bulldozers, and men hanging from wires
stretched across the road.
The demolition of trees.
Cones and barricades on a road
where, once, a car stopped
in front of me to watch,

off to the side, four police pointing their guns
at a man, his hands pulling the air between
heaven and earth to him. I wanted to honk,
encourage the car to get moving,
I didn't want to get shot, accidentally. At home I shook.

The worst crime my mother witnessed,
other than her knowledge that my father
paid to have sex with other men every weekend,
was my uncle who, after his
series of strokes, called daily, whispering
obscenities in her ear: *Mary, come fuck me.*
My mother!—an ox who could have plowed
the entire state with a yoke strapped to her back.

In Florida the weather
is unpredictable. This year: hot.
The year my mother died, 1991: wet and cool.
Now her grave is covered in mimosa,
a ground vine. This afternoon I watered
my flowers. I did not learn their names

until I realized that Mother would not be around
to remind me which are worth
keeping, and which ones are weeds.

Part Two

Arbor Day, 4ᵗʰ Grade

If I moved backward, I'd find a hole
filled with my father's words.
But here—
        if I dare to open the window—
I'll find him dead.

I keep my past in a box
as if there are more days waiting for me.

I try to keep the dog
from howling at the silence.

Here I am, standing next to trees
in my yard. Someday I will give
them my body. Even though

I've come so far, the curtains remain closed.
We each cling to our own past.

Here is the tree
my schoolmates and I planted
for Arbor Day: the shovels, the circle
we made, the hole, the water. Here is the prayer
for it to grow and keep growing.

One day perhaps I'll be invited back through the door.
I've never been far enough away from that tree

or from those lies. Here is the way

I want to remember it:
        a girl, her head bowed. And dirt,
                        cupped in her hands.

Big Pine Key

Five rinky-dink bodies, white sand,
clouds, the beach empty except me and my
four brothers—sand fleas that I can't shake off
my feet. In November I will become
the other side of ugly, school enemies
will ask, *Are you a boy?* But now sand crawls
into my bikini, scratching my body,
and my brothers' swords (palmetto fronds) whip
through air. It is Big Pine Key, summer,
and I'm barely a girl. My brothers think they're kings
of this beach. Youth is like a sunburn that lasts
all night long and into the next day. Most of the time
we're in our bedrooms in Sarasota,
marking with masking tape the lines others
dare not cross. But it is summer and I put all
four of my brothers inside one mason
jar, seal it, and carry the four devils in glass to the picnic
table, and the Australian pines sink deep
into the ground while four miniature boys
scream for help, push against the glass, and climb
on each others' shoulders to twist open
the lid. When I become an adult, I
will seldom return to the Keys. I will
dislike the white beach, its salt, its water
stinging my eyes, the sun peering at my body.
It's like my mother says, when she hands me
the hot dog: *Que sera, sera.*
It was a rented religion, and one day I'll
master indecision. And sleep, cradling the blue
lingering in the sky, the butterfly so baffled
that it dreams of its own sour elixir,
                                its wings in agony.

The State Forever Under Construction

My mother's porch is just one missed turn
of the vanishing swirl of childhood.
Orange reflectors, barricades, and
temporary lanes control the events

and gestures of my life. Like the first men
in my life, the construction is a reminder
of me not thinking ahead. Only one man
has said he'd stay forever. Look at the news:

I've made mistakes, and still the red sign
above the door begs me to hurl myself, again,
toward the man who loves me now.

I have not yet charged him to ride my days,
nor did I ask him to disguise his path.
Everything changes here: weather, the roads,
the houses, the men. Will this one want me,

and how fast I drive, as he says, forever?
Can this road continue beyond
the night? My mother's porch no longer hums,
and she cannot phone me from her coffin

or knock on my door to offer me tea
or a handful of daisies. Each morning I turn
to shut off the noise, but it's not my mother's voice.

It is a longer route I take to get to work
or to the store. It is a humming sadness.
Before I ran down this dirt road to him
I knew he had other women. Will I always have

this fear? What if I become one of those women
who wants her life to be a front porch
that never changes, a woman who will let the time
she has left pass beneath the dome light

of her car on the only highway
she can take to get home to him, headlights
swirling and aiming for the lines
that will keep us from collisions?

Say One Word To Me

My mother cannot catch
baby alligators, but that is, perhaps, because she is dead.

Before then, she had her chance,
      and every night I reminded her

that people were going to be inside my pajamas. Against
the back of my thigh,

she smacked one of my sister's baby dolls.
Each afternoon was like

baptism when I emerged from the school bus. Soon I was in
a bright green field, filled with
                bald cow skulls.

Our house was surrounded by some of the best
climbing trees I'd ever seen. Butterflies floated
                    toward my desperate
           touch. A loud voice

was a knock that sucked me back
down the tree trunks, and I realized I could not hide,
from God
                or my mother.
The fact that I wanted to catch the gray light,
caused my mother to frown.
She crumpled up
her eyes, grabbed my arm,
              Say one word to me—
her yanking was never in a good mood. My bed was a
prison of ruffles that dreamed of becoming

It could have been
a giant tree.

                                  the perfect Florida day—
the grass in the back yard,
lizards waving at my hair in a state of half-straight,
daring me
to unlatch my windows.
I could hear the voices
glued to my bed. Lace and bows stuck out of my ears
                         like horns.
          I've always been off-center,

and now it's as if I'm missing an eye
or a limb, but now, of course, my mother

cannot yell at me. She cannot even see me holding
this yellow light that
                      hangs from my fingers.

The Worship of Oranges

When I lived in Sarasota, I loved eating oranges off trees—
something about that double line of ragged, quiet
orange trees pruned into long arms and distorted bodies
appealed to me, a girl less girlish than her peers, and it taught me
about flavor and what sticks to the hands—the juice breaking free
from its cover. The television advertisements made
everyone want to taste my Florida. Strangers craved
something ultimately synthetic, pulpless,
smooth, and artificially sweetened.

Oh, those cruel blossoms of September,
the stench of chicken manure shoveled
carefully under trees at my father's demands, the weeding
he required and a hand-tilled four-foot circle of dirt beneath,
the pruning of lower branches exactly three feet
above ground. I was responsible for the supply of fruit
from eight trees. And now I buy my orange juice,
having moved away; at times, I prefer it
to the orange in my hand, its clinging dirt, its thin skin.

Here aisles shine, and boys wearing white
aprons lay oranges in rows on shelves covered with green plastic
carpet. It is easy to forget the way I carried
two dozen oranges from each tree to the bushel basket at the end
of the rows. Once there was a girl balancing a pile of chicken shit
on a shovel beneath an orange tree, dumping it, watching it
drop, stepping back. And the oranges worshiped her.

Cold War

There was proof of fear in 1970: beneath our desks,

where kids stuck their gum, we held onto
our knees, waiting for the bomb. Ten years passed,

and I grew to be afraid of tanks coming down
Lockwood Ridge Road and men with machine guns

knocking on my door. The odds suggested to me
it was time for us to take our share of machetes in our bedrooms.

Why didn't they take my son away from me?
I was not a good parent. He was

a bouncing ball in his desk at school. He failed
to understand the purpose of geometry. I was certain men

would come for me when I was in the shower, naked,
alone, my baby boy in the next room, asleep,

or they'd roll up the driveway at dinner between the pot roast
and mashed potatoes. Twenty more years, and now

I can't believe I still have all my fingers. What's stopping
my neighbor from slicing my head off? Planes fly over

and I wonder if fire will drop onto my rooftop,
if the boom of the shuttle re-entering our atmosphere

is really the big one, finally, coming to America.
I am after all, only sixty miles or so from Disney World,

our symbol of fun. Still, no tanks appear in my front yard
but I've seen the TV reports from war-ripped countries:

bullets flying between mothers and their children as they
walk to the market. I've grown afraid of the construction

workers across the street. Those hammers. Those nails
pinning shingles down to the roof. The men could

march over to my house and insist I turn over
to them my dried flowers, my postcards on the wall,

my notebooks, my pencils, my rocks collected from trips.
But what I'm really afraid of is that there won't be enough

rain for my wildflowers, lightning will strike my new TV,
I'll never learn to keep a clean house. Somewhere,

a place I've never been, a mother covers her child's body
like a blooming crimson bougainvillea vine.

Family Reunion

Each day I walk to the creek
knowing I long ago gave up my mother's heaven.

My family's reunion is taking place
fifty miles away
—a pig sliced open in honor

of an uncle, home from saving the world.

I'm certain the bruise on my knee
is a sunset. Why didn't I say this sooner—

The wasp behind my head is like the ladder in a nightmare.

The sun slices my yard toward the direction of spite.
Each day I hope daisies rise.

Even the dog stands there, eyeing the late afternoon.

I'm looking for a branch from which to hang
the laundry or maybe a cliff from which to throw
the entire basket of years.

Letter of Forgiveness

Instead of answering my mother, I listened to the radio,
climbed a tree into my room, lip-synched into the hairbrush.

My fame ran her ragged, and by the end of the day,

I had to take off, slide under my bed to hide
where I watched my mother's bare feet
wait for me to make a sound, like flies in a swarm.
I'll give you something to cry about.

Instead I laughed at her big toes. I poked at lint on the floor,
covered my mouth, and even though I didn't own chloroform,
I knew how to be silent.

Once I threw a green rock into the meadow. It knocked my mother out.
Once, before the sky went black, I held my father's drill like a gun.

When Mother's feet left my room, I pulled paper from my school notebook, wrote
an apology inside an envelope, and snuck it out, all the way to the mailbox.

Later in the kitchen, I told my mother to fetch
the mail. I didn't know she was afraid of losing me, of losing
all her children to the man she married, the man she hated.

She obeyed me—walked down the half-mile driveway,
pulled out my letter. I watched from the living room window,

and dinner boiled, once again, in the kitchen pots.

Sundays

The oaks are twisted, their branches
hiding the owl. On Sundays, girls wore
dresses; boys wore good pants and good

shoes. We were not going to church
to hunt or fish or play games. It was *be quiet*
or get swatted with your mother's folded

hands. Now, instead of church on Sundays,
I go to the bookstore, mow the weeds in my
yard, wait for rain, listen to my neighbor

put trees through his mulch machine, or hope
for a drop in temperature. Sometimes
I listen to the blue jay in my yard shoot

his mock scream toward the hawks,
demanding they leave this area right now.
Cardinals join him, but the owl waits

while it is decided who must go and who may
stay. In church when I was a girl it seems
the adults talked of boats and angels. I was not

dreaming. My body sank into the roots
and dirt of scrub, but I could not see blackness.
I'm afraid I gave all my girlishness away

because my face was desperate
to be cradled. And now cardinals join
the jay—it's more than beating the drums.

It's a tattling wire strung across the entire
yard. I like to pretend fruit trees have filled
my memory and that Mother was less

a watchman and more like lantana spreading
across the state. Everyone folded their knives
before church and tucked

their guns inside their trucks. We were
camouflaged in the pews, stabbing the Bible
with our small fingers, covering ourselves

with clasped hands, pulled down into water,
and now I wait for the owl to make his final decision:
stay and listen to this nonsense, or fly.

Interlude

The Truth About Florida

I.

Yes, we have coastal plains, we have limestone,
pine uplands, hardwood hammocks, and beaches beaches beaches.
We have sugar cane, turf farms, oranges, and shrimp.

And theme parks: Disney World, China Land,
Holy Land Experience, but no Hurricane World.

We have *Celebration*—a real town made by Disney
where neighbors live in their own private enlightenment
and a deer—real/imagined/one of Bambi's offspring?—greets you at the
   entrance.

And we have other planned communities—some gated,
some not. Perhaps you'll see garage doors open wide,
tables spring up in driveways,
the owners selling Bibles, broken cribs,
a dining room table with three chairs,
a bicycle missing a chain.

We have more than a dozen motels named *The Sea Shell*.
We have a state prison named *Liberty Correctional Facility*.

II.

We water our passionflowers, but only on Thursdays and Sundays
as the law allows, and only before 10:00 a.m. or after 4:00 p.m.
The aquifer beneath us is drying up, and every year more
sinkholes swallow our trees, our houses, our cars.

One year, a car dealership fell into the sand
It became a festival, a carnival—hot dogs for sale, balloons,
T-shirts!—and at the bottom of the sinkhole
(three-hundred-twenty feet wide, ninety feet deep):
an old woman's house and dozens of crushed Porsches.

III.

In September 1969, when I started fifth grade,
my daddy said, *Just our luck*, because across the room
was the bussed-in face of George and other kids
whose dark skin looked smoother
than the words printed in my book.

Mrs. Darcy was reading again
from Genesis, because even though
we were in a public school,
it was her duty, she said, to teach us
the word of God.

She paced in front, holding the big book
in one hand, raising and lowering
her other hand for emphasis on sin and evil

and Eve tempting Adam with that apple,
and then the note in my hand, having been shipped
across the sea of white faces:
      I like you.
         George.

IV.

It rains here.
Portions of torn-up
railroad lines have become bike paths
for those who can tolerate the heat.
Most of us stay inside and watch
plastic flamingos in our yards.

We have one man who rides his lawn mower
with his belly showing. Wood storks mosey

along roadsides. Over their heads,
as they muddle through water, their bills
make circles on an evaporating calendar.

The sky is a canyon of heavy breath.

V.

At the Florida/Georgia border:
clouds, rain, and free orange juice.
And down the center more registered
hate groups than in any other state.

I try to believe there are more than two otters left
in our state parks. Household trash walks right into our swamps,
pulling the plug on raccoons and snakes.

We burn crosses in our neighbors' yards, and we believe
we have the right to carry guns in holsters.
We shoot our neighbors for not
putting the garbage on the curb.

If you move here, you must paint your house
only in the colors approved
by the Home Owners' Association (earth pastels are best).

And you must have the code at the gate.

Part Three

Some Women

Could you be seduced without those women who start storms,
who fly above desks, who cling to wallpaper—those girls

who arrange their hair twelve times each day as if a hairpin
will save their necks? Some women have exceptional ways to note

the scars they collected as girls. Some women locked their bodies away,
as if a body could be a little wooden box sanded down and shellacked.

Some women found this to be a better choice. Put a lid on that face,
look the other way, are you a boy or a girl, is there suicide in your fingers?

Some women accumulate dog bites, while others are given acid
for their faces, bruises for the empty pots on their cheeks. Some women

are electric sockets. Some women are wings with skin, some blush
with fingers laced in glass. Did you get that memo? I scratch

the napkin on my eyelid as if it is a blade of grass, I mouth words into
a snake's fangs. Some women take heaven apart and disappear into a storm.

Protection

Oak pollen from every tree
in the state is piled in my driveway.
My dog prefers to walk without her leash
in the mornings.

It seems we left long ago.

The air is humid, the sky blue,
no rain. A new rug in a room before we left—
a pillow, a dog's fur, a blanket of sand,
mail left untouched from yesterday.

Along our walk, a woman is vacuuming
oak leaves from her yard: a yard-wife gathering
the insides for a pillow or a bed of leaves.
A truck rounds the corner. A bird nest drops
from the sky—I imagine the last young
bird scratching itself on the edges
of its egg as it pulled out. Two unfenced dogs
cross the street, and my dog's mid-back rises
like bacon from a frying pan. The nest
must have lost its hold
on the tree branch—the mother bird's spit
having held the lichen on the outside
for protection like a helmet. Now the day
is lost before it opens.

The Three Dancers

Eyes rattle on paper plates
in swirls of crayons and markers
and words I do not understand,

words written by homeless children:
Sad is yellow one says—
another: *don't like you*
with two tear droplets in glitter-glue and yellow
pipe cleaner encircling it
just in case I forget how much she cried
when her brother's fist came to her face.

The purple dips
into the bottom O of the paper plate,
where the young painter's words remind me
that *lost is blue mixed up with yellow.*

Children are willing to give everything away.

Then there are vases of flowers and an old
photograph of me: I sit on the ground
between two standing girls—
my arms draped through a pillory at a theme park,
my tongue hanging out to appear exhausted,
my friend Tammy in her hip-huggers turning
her face, again, from the camera,
my cousin Christy—a showgirl
pointing out my plight.

We were fifteen-year-old virgins on the edge,
waiting for our lives to get started,
or hoping
at the very least
not to wither away.

It never occurred to us that we would become nothing
to each other,
our arms spreading out,
each of us headed toward our own yellow emptiness.

Children Without Their Own Beds

At home, the woods are dense, tangled
branches of scrub oak and saw palmettos,
and beyond that, there are children without
their own beds. Their eyes and hands line
the hallway of the homeless shelter.

I'm never sure where to stand—
woodlands or marsh, but always it is like a dream:
a waterfall, unsure of its own destination.
Rain stumbles across the pond,
or is it a child roaming just above the ground
where it is probably not safe enough
to walk? I had thought today would be filled
with walking, but the rain made its way back
in time to soak my body, and I crawled
toward my room, safe from water. If only
I could take one of them into my arms.
But I would rather take them all home—
beyond this marsh where I stand, where herons,
hawks, and ibis become my nightshade.

The children have been taken away
from what keeps us hidden from each other: a home.
Sleep is my own bed floating below me, but for them,
it is a matchbox that might catch fire any minute.
If the crows are laughing, they are laughing at all the empty
rooms, the children with no stories. When I visit them
at the shelter, they never ask me to stay
or to go. I exist only when I'm standing in the same emptiness
with them—after all, to them, my house is invisible,
and even if I could show them
the sunset as it turns to the color of hope,

even though I might claim
to be the opening in their fence,
even though I tell their stories,
it is only if someone begs to know them.

The Envelope

This house could be a string of laughter.
There could be lanterns or a glass jar.

You could find a meaning in a ring beneath a mattress,

or you could frame the butterflies from childhood
like beads of wildflowers along the highway.

You remember the leaves sinking beneath the sign
at a trailhead you visited last year,

and now minutes watch the pillow where you try to sleep.

Your day has amounted to nothing
except newspaper clippings in an unsealed envelope.

Near Dusk

It's not the first time I've walked in woods
with my son, now thirty-two, who squats
like a frog about to hop off the log's edge.
It's not the first time he's pointed out
the black-winged damselfly,
not the first time I've leapt back to his childhood:
the schoolyards where we hunted for bugs
near dusk, the trails in deep woods,
the swamps we slogged through,
the creek near our old house, both of us barefooted—
I was too young, in my early twenties.
We were both carrying nets, walking past snakes,
minnows, bluegills, in hopes of catching
crawfish, or whatever he was looking for
back then. I was looking for where we'd turn
around, go back home. Today the sky

tastes gray, like clouds, and the creek water
protects these fallen trees from the heavy winds
that have come with the rain this year.
I push through spiderwebs, my dog's leash,
and my wet dog jingles as she catches
up with us after stopping to smell something
I cannot. Here, at this point, the creek takes

a sharp turn, and mussel shells along the bed—
some black, some silver, some white—
catch my son's fingers and even here,
at the creek bed, I can't quite understand
his explanation of how they got here. I'm too busy
thinking about whether or not he'll be here
still next year—the taste of this world too much
for his fragile mind. He is too old for the silliness
of cradling him in my arms.

We walk again, and jump over trees
that have fallen across the trail, we ignore
the log across the creek where I once fell and broke
my wrist, called my son to rescue me. The muck
—from days of rain and the many bicyclists
who pass us in quick wind—reminds me
that I'm in too deep again, too close
to my son's explanations of fungus, how it lives
and grows in a world that does not like to see
defects or imperfection. My son is now farther
up the trail where the trees refuse
to keep standing, but here we are,

near dusk.

As a Child You Learn

You learn to be vigilant in spring

and you watch the boys and girls soar
outside your window as they perform a ballet

in the trees. This is important:
walk with lace wrapped around

your fingers   step carefully without making
too many knots. The sky covers everything:

your foot   your ankle
     your knees   your hands (your entire

body)—and even if you slip you need not understand
the wave that comes without warning. No.

You sit down   you
pick up grains of sand in the crevices

of the sidewalk with your fingertips
and you bow your tiny head.

Part Four

Map of My Room

There's no mirror in this room
to melt the air,

so I watch the wind
float past the window

or stare at the black postcards that keep
landing on the wall. This room

was once an anchored boat,
and I was shaken by the words

pinned against my chest.
Now I wait to be

struck by the wing of a sandhill crane
coming from the mouth of the sky,

but waiting like this blinds me.

I cannot see the house where dirty
laundry weeps on the floor.

The cranes stand knee-deep in water,
or is it my mind,

and I cannot think of what it is beneath
us that hums and taps its own fingers

as if water were a drum or a sleeve
anxious to be tucked into its own life.

Landscape

*"All thoughts vanish into emptiness,
like the imprint of a bird in the sky."*

—Chogyam Trunga

In the animal hours of night
deer shadows appear,
their cries rise like distance.

Then morning, and wrens
are building their nest
in a moment that cuts into my memory of an old porch.
Yellow frostweeds sway like capes floating

in a canoe. Roselings sprout
from sand. Blue sailboats across
                        the midday sky.

Evening, I walk to the river for sunset,
it might remind me of
a girl who can still track deer
or mice or blood.

The wrens do not care
where this path leads, or my palm
that is always moving toward death.

Soldier's Creek Trail

She moves her hands along the trail
as if they are waves of birds
without knowing that down at the edge
where water meets sand, darkness
peeks out from behind roots.
She often wonders if she matters, but not here
where walking each day
her fingers find traces
of seed in her pockets.

She knows there is pollen on the ground.
She knows the flowers coming from the dead trunk up ahead
will soon form on her forehead.
She must look into the palm of her hand
or into this branch
which appears far away from the path,
and now she's kissing the ground and waiting
to speak, but perhaps she won't even remember
the creek, the bending copper that sings.
I have come this far, she reminds herself,
even if it doesn't seem so.

The woods offer her a log
across the creek where she could watch children,
if they were present, contradict the silence
among oaks and pines and palms. Time crosses the creek
and, just as she turns to face the ferns, she slips and becomes
a penny tossed into the water, her wrist shattered,
and she thought it couldn't hurt—
this walking all the way back,
even though she couldn't see where
she was going—a mirror of what had come
before appeared as though others
were on the trail with her—away from the light and the ferns.

Instead of this tree, it's as if
she is lifted across the creek—not the fingers
of her right hand folded into these roots
along the bank: a sling carving out her name.

Invisible Week

Moss hangs from oak trees
as if fall does not exist,

as if trees are mirrors of
previous years.

Smoke quivers
like damp hands
closing over a stone.

This week is a tired train—

a spiderweb is the final
mystery of the lamppost.

Seven dark evenings
and only the memory of wind
drifts past the window.

Here, private fingers and lips
no longer place wishes upon

the window where a dog's tongue
and breath linger on the pane—

faint imprints of hope.

Mud Song

I found the hollowed-out wind, a thin
unreadable sign,
and, for three hours, I hiked the muddied path—
bright palmettos, armadillo holes, dog shit.

Each step was still a desperate rerun of childhood.
I, the oldest girl, did not become a thin tugboat,
as predicted, floating along the horizon.

Though I'll never again see
my parents, their lives are nailed to mine.
Like their little girl of silver I wait for the call,
still angry at my hands, like pebbles, in the kitchen sink.
I caved into expectations, but never
stopped asking for daisies or gardenias.
I felt like a mournful twig.

Here, I could start dying. My head
falls onto the shag carpet
of my teenage room. I walk
as if I can no longer hear my parents.
I know the value
of mud on a dog's paw. I want to wake
and disappear into the minutes
where the crows fly.
I want someone
to leave me in the clouds
and carry my gown across the night.

Passion Flower

The vine loops itself through
the posts on the porch, and though it is October
and the purple flower will not appear until next
May, it would like to come inside.

When people first came to Florida it was all
woods and bugs and flowers that refused
to lift themselves from the sand.
Now someone comes

down the stairs, wanting to take
a picture of this family. And this is the only place

I want to be, where the rain surrounds the bed,
where once there was a thin wire that separated my yard
from my neighbor's.

One day I will see this house
from a distant window and wonder what
it's been through, and I'll say, "Where
is the woman who planted the vine?"

Even the new people will want to know
where all this color came from,
flowers rising from beneath their feet.

Window Seat

The cedar waxwings question
the virtues of loneliness from their sagging
pulpits in the trees, as if I am a silhouette against
their window.
          A bulldozer in the distance shatters

the air, but still the dried flowers in this vase anchor
the morning. And still I peer out toward the eye
of the staghorn's one leaf.
              This is almost the way
I like it—the window's mouth a smooth lamp,

but I keep losing my voice to distant cars
and the paper on my desk asks the varnished wind
a favor, as when warblers
fly away the moment they see my glass face.

Break Me

I have no charm or grace, not even a bag of radio static,
so let the winter begin, let the desert break out of its glass.

Others have slipped their timeless legs into the sea
when no one else watched or dropped bread on the floor.

I was never home or away from home, was never a glass of water,
but as a girl, I sang hymns while mowing grass on the tractor.

No one remembers my songs. Listen: the grass here has stopped growing!
I want to slink away into a basket of darkness,

old calendars, and bags I never carry. Once, I sat down,
away from the tree, unafraid, and when he carried me

over the river toward new songs I almost died of contentment.
I was a woman in need of grass and wind and brackish lagoons.

I always forget to bring my own flashlight,
I refuse the quarters and memories from the other side.

The day will go forward whether I agree with it or not.
Let me know when you can rattle the bones out of my hands

or my face. There are no hills here, but I know how to hang on
like a dead vine. I pile dirt into my mouth while the sun

tries to hold an entire day. Don't try to shake my arms.
Let me become roots of the tree—watch, as my hands turn into muck.

Florida Trail, Hopkins Prairie

The day moved like a mule playing a harp

each step on top of the pine straw
wrapped my old crimes—
my somber arm heard the song
of the tree covered in ash.

The sagging house became night,
a dream that unmasked

the borrowed jar. The prairie grass
is fog in the basket of morning,
the wind in the trees like traffic
too familiar—an old creed,

an old melody in the sand.

Beneath the grass I might find
the reason my hands
feel warning bumps near the edge
of a narrow road. My mind sparkles
like pitch memory—
a dog could be lost in the forest

or explain the mouth,
sorry for its music.

Woman at Park Near Lake Monroe

I fill my pockets with keys, plastic bags,
emptiness, and leave the house.

Bring me to cypress knees near water
where ferns thrive beneath uprooted trees.
Let me crawl up and over the ladder of the day.

Grass hides from a boy on a skateboard
charcoal rots in its bed.

I hold my own face like a cup,
unwritten words trapped in the sky,
and there is no way to hold myself up

while I am sinking into it.
Somewhere there is a mummy, dressed and encased in glass,
and I am the last woman who craves touch.

Remember the Night I Almost Threw Myself Off the Jetty into the Crashing Waves?

It was a beach where sharp edges
kept me hoping for at least two fish to call my name.

Remember those trees bragging
about the birds they'd held
in their branches earlier that day?

It was before I knew how to hold my own hand,
before I knew to make sure my shoes fit before walking.

My hands were blank
            like a white lamp.
My wrists were knotted.

I did not bother to rinse the saltwater and sand from my feet.

Part Five

Things to Do In Your 50s

Bury your bones deep in the back yard and wear pricey cotton collars.
Show your teeth when necessary. Refuse to open the door for anyone.
Don't look back.
Control panting to thirty minutes in public.
If you must eat potato chips, lick them off the floor.
Be proud of your nipples, even though they are more than visible.
While watching the sky from the earth, raise your arms and legs,
and feel the grass scratch your back.
Meditate even when you're not alone. When others are watching TV,
protect your space. Tongue your lover's face.
Learn to say no, even if it comes out as a howl.
Remember, you've chased enough snakes. You've done your share of sitting.
You've waited long hours for a single touch.
Eat grass when there's nothing else to do.
Be the first to announce anything—a knock at the door, a lizard
on the back porch, a friend disguised as a monster. Pay no attention to the
    love notes
rattling in your head. Roll in shit, mud puddles, wet paint, sand, dead squirrels.
Jump fences. Chase anything on wheels.
Dig holes where you can keep what you need for later: rope, Frisbee, stuffed
    monkey,
frozen bones, dead lizards, hope, tennis balls.
Don't let anyone force you off the chaise lounge.
Imagine you are human.

Walk or Fly, but Do Not Look Down

Pine cones fall on my head each day
when I collect my mail. I am not afraid of walking

down my street, but when I fly
in dreams, above buildings, I'm afraid of telephone wires,
afraid of dropping my arms

in order to dodge the hundreds of lines
that block my flight.

I've never been afraid of climbing trees.

Do not warn me of coffee grounds or pebbles.
Do not shred the curtains or teach me to fold towels.
I am not afraid of sleeping or waking.

I'm not afraid of unlocked doors, I'm afraid of windows open at night.
I'm not afraid of blankets, I'm afraid of a pillow pushed onto my face.
I'm not afraid of my swimming pool, I'm afraid of tidal waves.

I am always waiting for lemons to fall from the tree.

I am not afraid of hurricanes.
Here I am walking on the dark street toward thunder.

Is there anything to fear in a universe that hums like this?

Tonight

       seems like darts flashing in a tunnel
the days are often empty   and then

through this breath child opens her hands
through this breath a chickadee waits
through this breath through this breath

dirt and worms became family
in your hands

you bear all you can in each breath
a whip you feel as you sleep
a spur in your foot walking in dreams
but you will not die in these woods

we all know   there are no words

—for A.S.

When Those Days Come

She had a retreat in the house
by the pond. It was her life,
and then she had gone
outside, just to watch
the frogs, to sit under
the pine tree. She tapped
the palmettos on her way,
point to point, and nodded
like a girl undressing
for a bath. Each day she convinced

herself it was her life because one day
she would become an old woman,
the one whose wrists will have to be held,
the one wanting soup. Her blessed room
was unread, a clearing
of darkness, a bottom lip torn
and ragged, filled with salt
and memories of grilled vegetables.

When those days come, the yard—
that had sworn years before to be her trumpet,
to be her church—will die.
The house will cling
to the suspended pines. Dirt will be
a mirror that shows a hand
no longer reaching into it.

Moon, Stars

I have watched the soaked moon
I have tried to hold down my house

tried to sew a lid on this street
On this trip to town I hold

water in my cupped palms—
the dead baby I always forget

I do not wish to sleep on the porch
the stars I see in the sky, already gone

In Memory of Me

The rocks are not for pulling my body to the bottom of the sea,
but for guests to hold in their hands while the day continues to drip

with sunlight. I have become hay become wind become sour.
My hands feel as though they are draped from the top limb

of the camphor tree that stood outside my window, like a curtain
through my days of grading papers. Now the others speak:

Once, she was a lightbulb hanging from the basement ceiling.

She was a line on a single note card.

We were her friends until that night at dinner
when she spoke of marrying her dog.

Her silence no longer opens doors.

> *She listens only to the nest in the wild water.*

Permanence

I stood in the street moving dust
with my shoe, covering
the unwanted leaves. I wanted to walk farther,
sway toward the edge of something, but it was
the sturdy fence that brought me this open hand,
and I thought:
Give me the doll I mutilated
when I was a girl:
permanent marker in my hands,
I drew black
lines around her wrists
and shins, black lines from her
navel through her crotch to the small
of her back. And now, when I wait for
lights to pass or clouds to remind me
of a dress I once owned,
the leash pulls me back
toward a name I could easily forget.
Sometimes I try to live
as a woman facing these years,
yet here I stand begging for night
on a road of sand and leaves,
and from the darkness
threaded below me, I step down,
whisper the name of a tree. As a girl I slept
in my room and each morning
I woke as a doll with lines
drawn across my chest. I had forgotten
to whisper my name into the night. I grew
into a woman and forgot, while the sky
turned to sandstone.

The Oldest Plant in the Yard Speaks: Spicy Jatropha

We hear the red comments from the mirror:
the water caught in the rim of an upturned bucket.

Still we stand in the yard. Never as neat as folded dress shirts,
but vibrant like sky mixed with blood.

The stem of the bougainvillea reaches
for our right arms, and soon we will be more pale than the street.

Each day is inclined to ignore us, and each day is an endless maze.
Perhaps someone will go with us into the wise room of dusk.

Pagan Shoes

Picture frames are falling off my face
like oak leaves from the past fifty years
surrounding hands that do not look like mine.

I remain locked away from the sky
and its four corners like the summer of Florida
begging me to drag myself home.

I left yesterday's water on the windowsill
which suffers from clarity. It's true

that I'd jump off a bridge.
It's true that it no longer frightens me
to slip in the cracks where the ghosts
of men who wanted me dead
now live. I think of some angry movie I went to as a child

and without the title, without the plot or
the characters, the past leaves me
looking out the window
which is empty and restless

even though the fan blows on my face
and I remember that I could climb up to the roof
or run into the neighbor's yard. But these hands
cannot be mine. Back when I rode

the wagon across the driveway,
I knew our family's secrets were

mine to keep. I knew my brothers were my
best friends. There is no longer a preacher calling me
up the aisle, though as a child I floated up at least five times—
just to be safe. I stare at my face

but I have disappeared. These hands are not mine.
I wear pagan shoes now, and I stare
at the trees I wish I could still climb. I live

beneath a blanket
which is all wrong, my shoes
screeching like they do, pointed and dying,
trying to sneak out,
trying to do wrong without me.

Postlude

Terry Reminds Herself How to Live

Wear a mood ring with the hope of understanding yourself.
Take recyclables out only on weeks you feel like it, and,
Jesus Christ, remember your name. Plant

Red Sisters—*Dracaena; Cordyline terminalis*—outside
your window where the dog
once trotted. Ignore phone calls

from your sister and long-lost cousins
you didn't speak to as a child. Dream about the boy
you liked in middle school—
the one with dark hair and no smile. Leave your notebook

with lists and lists of things to do
in a public bathroom
an hour from your house. Write checks to yourself

for large amounts, but never cash them.
After you've learned the names
of all the dogs on your street, run along the side
of their fence and dance with them.

Buy two pair of glasses:
one for downstairs and the other
for upstairs. Believe in nothing
—not even the bricks you stacked outside six months
ago for the garden walkway. Keep dried flowers close to you.

Save a rock from every path you walk down.

When your mother's photo stares at you from the basket,
remind her that she is dead.

Never sing in public.
Never pay more than four dollars for a slice of cake.
Don't clean house.

Forget the gardenia you tried to grow
in memory of your mother; use the dirt from the pot
for another, more willing, plant. Remember the dog
that lived next door looking at you
from the low window, waiting for you to open
the door and say her name.

Acknowledgments

Grateful acknowledgments to the editors of the following journals where many of these poems first appeared.

580 Split: "Mud Song"; "In Memory of Me"
Adirondack Review: "The Three Dancers"
Appalachian Heritage: "When Those Days Come"
Arabesques Review: "Cold War"
Ascent: "Family Reunion"
BlazeVOX online: "Escape"; "Map of My Room"; "Dead Owl"
Borderlands: Texas Poetry Review: "The Worship of Oranges"
Cimarron Review: "The State Forever Under Construction"
Cold Mountain Review: "Window Seat"
Connotation Press: An Online Artifact: "Walk or Fly, But Do Not Look Down"; "Afternoon Forecast"; "Arbor Day, 1967"
Earth's Daughters: "Passion Flower"
Flint Hills Review: "The Woman Reminds Herself How to Live"
Flyway: "Sundays"
Foliate Oak: "Road Rage"
Forge: "Alligators"
Fourth River: "Drought"
Ginosko: "Obedience"; "The Truth About Florida"
Lime Hawk: "Some Women"
Main Street Rag: "Invisible Week"
Painted Bride Quarterly: "Big Pine Key, Summer 1974"
Pantheon Magazine: "Florida Survival Guide"; "Say One Word To Me"
Raleigh Review: "Soldier's Creek Trail"
Rattle: "What Remains"
Stoneboat: "Letter of Forgiveness"
Zocalo Public Square: "Near Dusk"

Deepest gratitude to Debbie Weaver for her care and attention to the manuscript. Many thanks to Katie Riegel and Laurie Uttich who read early and late drafts of these poems. Thanks to Lisa Ahrens and Barbara Smith-Mandell at Truman State University Press.

Special thanks to Don Stap.